The Cost

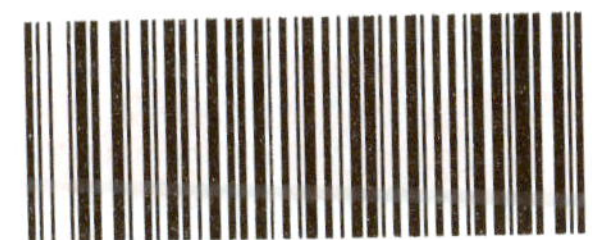

by Iris L

illustrated by Cheryl Mendenhall

 HOUGHTON MIFFLIN BOSTON

Printed in India

ISBN-13: 978-0-547-01870-6
ISBN-10: 0-547-01870-3

2 3 4 5 6 7 8 9 0940 15 14 13 12 11 10

The cat looks in the box.
He puts on the hat.

The dog looks in the box.
She puts on the cape.

The bear looks in the box.
He puts on the boots.

The fox looks in the box.
She puts on the skirt.

The lion looks in the box.
He puts on the crown!

Responding

TARGET SKILL Understanding Characters

Characters A bear and a lion are characters in this story. What do they do? What does this tell you about them? Make a chart.

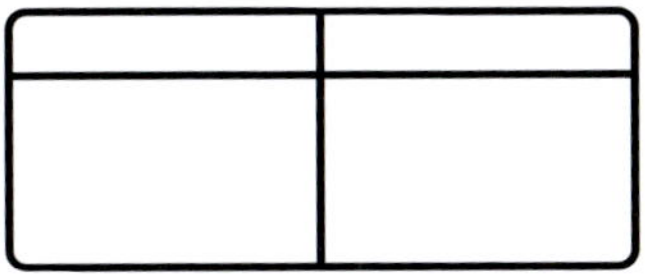

Write About It

Text to Text Write about another book you have read about costumes. Tell what happened in the beginning, middle, and end.

do	**look**
down	**off**
have	**out**
help	**take**

TARGET SKILL **Understanding Characters** Tell more about characters.

TARGET STRATEGY **Summarize** Stop to tell important events as you read.

GENRE **Fiction** is a story that is made up.